D1218347

FRONTLINE WORKERS DURING COVID-19

by Kerry Dinmont

BrightPoint Press

San Diego, CA

BrightP◇int Press

© 2021 BrightPoint Press
an imprint of ReferencePoint Press, Inc.
Printed in the United States

For more information, contact:
BrightPoint Press
PO Box 27779
San Diego, CA 92198
www.BrightPointPress.com

LIBRARY OF CONGRESS CATALOGING-IN-PUBLICATION DATA

Names: Dinmont, Kerry, author.
Title: Frontline workers during COVID-19 / by Kerry Dinmont.
Description: San Diego, CA : BrightPoint Press, [2021] | Series: The COVID-19 pandemic | Includes bibliographical references and index. | Audience: Grades 7-9
Identifiers: LCCN 2020050558 (print) | LCCN 2020050559 (eBook) | ISBN 9781678200626 (hardcover) | ISBN 9781678200633 (eBook)
Subjects: LCSH: COVID-19 (Disease)--United States--Juvenile literature. | Medical personnel--United States--Juvenile literature. | Service industries workers--United States--Juvenile literature.
Classification: LCC RA644.C67 D56 2021 (print) | LCC RA644.C67 (eBook) | DDC 362.1962/41400973--dc23
LC record available at https://lccn.loc.gov/2020050558
LC eBook record available at https://lccn.loc.gov/2020050559

CONTENTS

AT A GLANCE

- COVID-19 is caused by a virus that was first discovered in China in December 2019. It soon became a global pandemic.

- COVID-19 spreads primarily through the air.

- Frontline workers included first responders, health care workers, store clerks, truck drivers, custodians, maintenance workers, and more. They had to keep working during the pandemic and were at a higher risk of getting COVID-19.

- Frontline workers could get the virus from customers, coworkers, or patients. It could be hard to keep a safe distance.

- Personal protective equipment (PPE) helped protect frontline workers. PPE includes N95 respirators, surgical masks, face shields, surgical gowns, and gloves.

- Most frontline workers earned less money than the average American worker. They could not afford to stay home if they felt sick.

- Some politicians tried to make laws that gave frontline workers hazard pay. Hazard pay would help compensate for the risks that workers took by coming into work.

- Some people made cloth masks to donate to hospitals. Students volunteered to provide childcare for frontline workers. Other people handled grocery shopping for health care workers.

WHO ARE FRONTLINE WORKERS?

Marie Deus woke up before sunrise on an April day in 2020. The sixty-five-year-old left the house at about 5:00 a.m. She got on the bus and went to work.

Deus was born in Haiti. At the age of twenty, she moved to the United States.

Hospital workers were at a high risk of becoming sick with COVID-19.

Deus had worked in a hospital kitchen

for the past fifteen years. She brought

meals to patients who couldn't get food

for themselves.

Because she worked at a hospital, Deus was considered a frontline worker. Frontline workers had important jobs that **exposed** them to the public. They still had to go into work during the COVID-19 **pandemic**. This deadly disease was first discovered in China in December 2019. Since then, many people around the world had gotten sick. Because frontline workers had to go into work, they were at higher risk of being exposed to COVID-19. They had close contact with people and surfaces that might be contaminated with the virus.

Coughing is common for those sick with COVID-19.

The past few days, Deus had been tired. She was sneezing. Deus thought she just had allergies. She took a couple of days off work. But now she was going back. She always worried she might lose her job. She was older than many of her coworkers. Deus didn't speak perfect English. Her friend Daniel Joseph said, "She knew, if you can't come to work, sooner or later you may be losing your job."[1] Deus walked into the building. Before reaching the spot to get checked for COVID-19 **symptoms**, she collapsed.

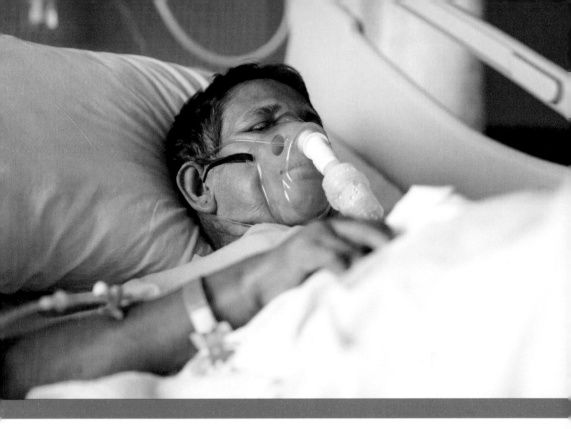

Health care workers may give oxygen through a mask to patients who are having trouble breathing.

An emergency room team rushed a stretcher to her. Deus needed oxygen. A doctor put her on a ventilator. This machine helps people breathe. After a few weeks on the ventilator, Deus did not improve.

Truck drivers continued to work and make deliveries throughout the pandemic.

She died in late April. She was one of many frontline workers who lost their lives to COVID-19.

Health care workers were among the most commonly recognized frontline workers. But there were many others. First responders and store clerks were in this group. So were truck drivers, janitors, and garbage collectors. These people were often praised as heroes. But many had no choice. They needed to work in order to support themselves and their families.

CHAPTER ONE

HOW WERE FRONTLINE WORKERS AT HIGH RISK?

COVID-19 spreads quickly. Common symptoms of COVID-19 include coughing and loss of smell. But people can be **contagious** before they realize they are sick. By late 2020, health experts estimated that 0.6 percent of people infected with

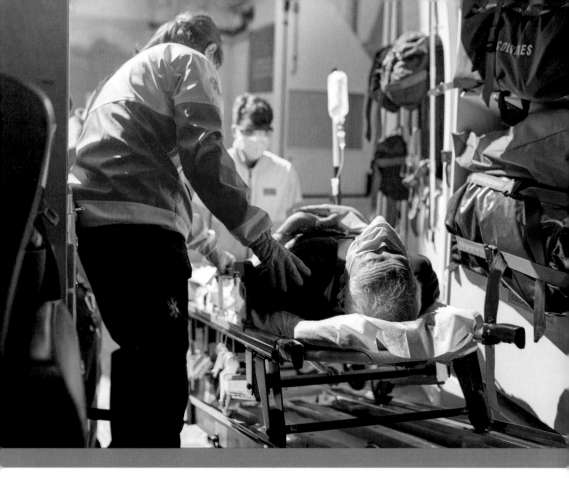

People sick with COVID-19 may be rushed to the hospital if they are having difficulty breathing.

COVID-19 died. Even more needed urgent care at hospitals. Health care workers were quickly overwhelmed.

The pandemic disrupted daily life. Around the world, people tried to slow the spread of the disease. Governments ordered

some businesses to temporarily close.

People worked from home when possible.

But people still needed food, medicine,

and health care. Frontline workers had to

keep working.

TRUCK DRIVERS

Truck drivers bring food to grocery stores and supplies to hospitals. They often rely on restaurants to get meals. In March 2020, many states ordered restaurants to close. Only drive-throughs could stay open. But large trucks cannot go through drive-throughs. And usually people on foot cannot order at the window. To help truck drivers, some restaurant workers ignored this policy. At other places, truckers had to ask people in cars to order the food for them.

Frontline workers often interact with a lot of people. This made it more likely for them to be exposed to COVID-19. The virus that causes the disease spreads mainly through the air. Sneezing, coughing, or talking can cause droplets that contain the virus to spread into the air. People nearby may inhale the droplets. They can get sick. Doctors recommended that people stay at least 6 feet (1.8 m) away from each other in public. This distance made it more difficult for droplets of the virus to spread. But frontline workers couldn't always stay that far from customers.

The virus can also stay on surfaces for a period of time. If people touch the surface and then touch their eyes, nose, or mouth, they could get sick. But this is an uncommon way for the virus to spread.

FARMERS' RISK

Farmers kept working through the pandemic. People still needed food. Since they often work outdoors away from other people, their risk of getting COVID-19 was relatively low. But they were affected in other ways. More people were eating at home, and they ate fewer vegetables than they would when eating at a restaurant. This meant farmers had more vegetables than people were buying. Farmers sold less vegetables than usual.

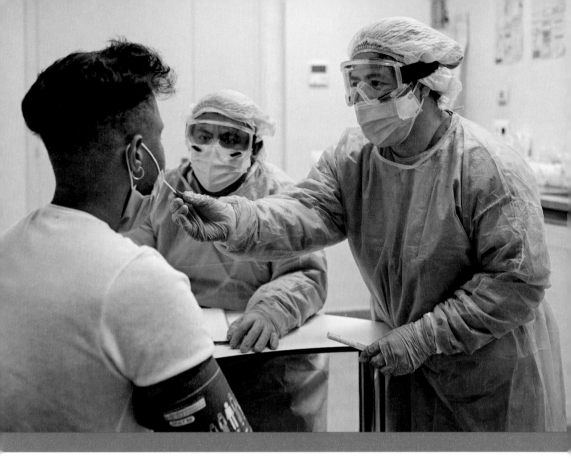

Health care workers wear protective equipment to keep them safe from the virus.

DIRECT EXPOSURE

Some frontline workers had direct

contact with COVID-19 patients. These

included health care workers such as

doctors, nurses, paramedics, and staff

at nursing homes. They wore personal protective equipment (PPE) such as masks and gloves. PPE protects the wearers from getting sick. It keeps droplets from entering the nose and mouth. But even with PPE, health care workers were three times more likely than the public to get COVID-19.

People could also get COVID-19 from coworkers. They might have to work close together for long periods of time. Even if both people were wearing masks, the risk of exposure increased as they spent more time together. For example, a veterinary assistant may need to restrain a dog or cat.

Veterinarians may have to work together when caring for an animal. The virus may spread among coworkers.

A nearby veterinary technician draws blood.

They couldn't be 6 feet apart. If one of them

was sick, the other could become sick

as well.

COMPANY PRIVACY POLICIES

Sometimes a frontline worker would test positive for COVID-19. They might have worked closely with coworkers. The US Centers for Disease Control and Prevention (CDC) said that sick employees should not come to work. Privacy rules mean that employers cannot tell employees who is sick. But the CDC did say that employers should tell employees if someone they have worked with gets COVID-19. That way employees could take precautions. They could quarantine, or stay at home, for fourteen days until they knew if they were

Physical barriers helped prevent the virus from spreading among coworkers.

sick or not. This would stop them from

infecting others. The employees could also

get tested to see if they were infected.

However, sometimes companies didn't

tell workers when people in the workplace

had the virus. There was no law requiring

them to do so. **Custodians** in particular were often not informed. The *New York Times* interviewed several janitors. Many were not told whether they were cleaning an area that had been used by someone with COVID-19. This made it harder for them to keep from getting sick themselves.

Some custodians work for schools with multiple campuses. Custodians may be moved between campuses. Sometimes a campus was shut down because of COVID-19. The custodians there were sent to an active campus. They worked with new people. Custodian Lupe Espinoza said,

Custodians cleaned surfaces that could have droplets of the virus.

"What I've seen on my team is . . . people from this school being sent to schools that were shut down after quarantine. . . . And I also received somebody from a school that was shut down."[2] Some custodians said they were being exposed to more people than necessary. They also thought that moving workers like that helped the virus spread.

INDIRECT EXPOSURE

Some frontline workers help customers. Customers could have COVID-19 without knowing it. Pharmacists help people get medication. Grocery store clerks often cannot stay 6 feet away from customers. Clerks touch the same items a customer has selected to purchase. Clerks and pharmacists may take customers' credit cards or money. The virus could be on

Frontline workers could get sick from handling objects such as credit cards. Droplets of the virus could be on these objects.

these objects. If workers touch their faces

after handling these items, they could

get sick.

People on public transportation could get sick from other passengers or dirty surfaces.

Frontline workers didn't only experience

risks at work. Commuting to work could

also be risky. Some workers needed

to take the bus, the subway, or other

public transportation to work. It could be

hard to stay 6 feet away from people in these places. Some passengers didn't wear masks. Using public transportation increased people's risk of getting COVID-19. However, the workplace was still where people were more likely to get sick.

Frontline workers provided important services during the pandemic. While some people worked from home, frontline workers went into work every day. There were some things they could do to protect themselves. But their jobs put them at a greater risk of getting the virus.

CHAPTER TWO

HOW DO FRONTLINE WORKERS PROTECT THEMSELVES?

Some frontline workers used PPE to reduce their chances of getting COVID-19. This equipment helps block the virus from entering the wearer's body. PPE includes N95 respirators, surgical

There were many types of PPE that frontline workers could use to protect themselves.

masks, face shields, surgical gowns,

and gloves.

TYPES OF PPE

N95 respirators were important PPE. These

masks block 95 percent of small particles,

N95 masks were important forms of PPE for health care workers.

including virus droplets. In addition, these

masks make a tight seal around the nose

and mouth. These masks filter both inhaled

and exhaled air.

Surgical masks also filter particles. But they fit loosely. They do not make an airtight seal. Inhaled air is not completely filtered. For this reason, they are not as effective as N95 masks at protecting against COVID-19. However, they do help prevent someone with COVID-19 from spreading the disease. Surgical masks help block droplets carrying the virus from getting into the air. This protects nearby people from getting sick.

A face shield covers a person's whole face. It does not filter air. It does little to stop a person from breathing in the virus. But the shield blocks droplets from landing on

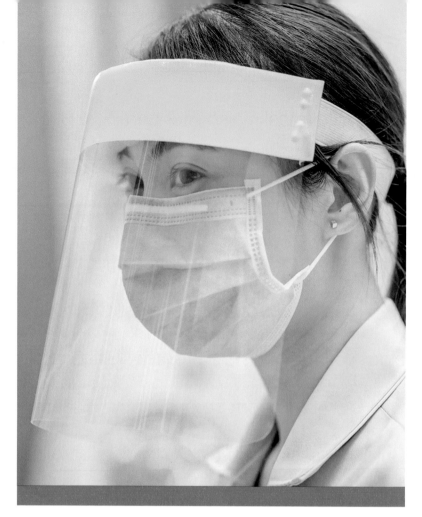

Face shields help stop droplets from landing on the face. Masks keep the virus from spreading to others.

the wearer's face and eyes. Shields also

keep people from touching their faces.

If someone touched his or her face with

unwashed hands, the virus could enter that

person's nose or mouth. This could make the person more likely to get sick.

Gowns and gloves protected health care workers from contact with the virus. Gloves and gowns are supposed to be thrown away after each use. Doing this keeps health care workers from spreading the virus among patients.

PPE SHORTAGES

The US **federal** government keeps a **stockpile** of PPE for emergencies. It did not have enough PPE at the beginning of the pandemic. The stockpile included just 1 percent of the masks needed for one year of a pandemic. The stockpile was quickly used up. In addition, the public was also scrambling to buy masks and gloves. Soon there was a shortage of PPE.

Because of this shortage, health care workers did not always have the PPE they needed. N95 masks should be thrown away after seeing each patient. But health care workers had to use N95 masks for whole days. This increased their risk of getting the virus. By July 2020, 87 percent of nurses had needed to reuse at least one type of single-use PPE. Emergency medical technicians were told to use only surgical

Companies needed to produce millions of masks to protect frontline workers and the public.

masks, even when caring for suspected COVID-19 patients. They could not use N95 masks because of the PPE shortages.

These shortages put extra stress on frontline workers. They worried about getting sick. Yvette Beatty worked as a home health aide during the pandemic.

She said of the shortage, "We are running around with no protective gear. I would love to see us have hazard masks, instead of putting cloths over our face or . . . buying dollar masks. We are taking a chance on our life, too. We need equipment."[3]

PPE was largely reserved for health care workers during the pandemic. Other

SHORTAGES CONTINUE

US companies stepped up during the PPE shortage. Some began making PPE. But after half a year, there was still a shortage. There was also an increase of counterfeit PPE products. These products did not protect workers. So hospitals preferred to buy from known companies who had been making PPE for a long time.

frontline workers did not have many options to protect themselves. Custodians needed PPE to perform their jobs even before COVID-19. They deal with chemicals that can damage the lungs, eyes, and skin. PPE shortages made their jobs riskier.

PROTECTING FRONTLINE WORKERS AND FAMILIES

Many frontline workers who did not work in health care had to use cloth masks. These masks provided some protection for the wearer. But cloth masks were more helpful when everyone wore them because the fabric blocked droplets. Frontline workers were at risk if people around them were not wearing masks. Some states and cities made mask **mandates** to protect frontline workers and the public. These laws required everyone to wear masks in public. In November 2020, thirty-seven states required masks in public.

Some stores limited the number of people from a household who could shop at one time. People need membership cards to shop at Costco. In April, Costco said only two people per membership card could enter their stores at once. That same month, Walmart limited the number of

MASKS OR FACE COVERINGS REQUIRED IN PUBLIC

NYS MANDATE

New York State was one of many US states that required people to wear masks while in public.

customers who could shop in their stores.

They did not want their stores to be too

crowded. These steps reduced the risk of

store employees getting sick at work.

Frontline workers needed to protect

themselves and their families. Many

health care workers worried that they

might bring the virus home to the people

they lived with. Some put their clothes in

the laundry as soon as they got home.

Then they immediately showered to remove

virus droplets.

MENTAL HEALTH RISKS

During the pandemic, many hospitals were overwhelmed with patients. Health care workers had to work long shifts. The conditions were stressful. Staff shortages meant that some people worked in situations they had little experience with. More of the patients they cared for were dying. Shortages of PPE added to that stress. Health care workers suffered from more mental health issues at this time. They dealt with anxiety, depression, and insomnia.

Other workers isolated themselves in their homes. They used a bedroom and bathroom that no one else used. But not everyone had multiple bathrooms. Some workers stayed in hotel rooms. Others stayed in campers or cars. A nurse in Oregon said, "I feel very guilty for not being there for my husband and child. . . . But I don't want to put them at risk."[4]

PPE was vital to protecting frontline workers. They took many steps to stay safe. But they still took risks to do their jobs.

CHAPTER THREE

HOW DID INCOME LEVEL AFFECT WORKERS?

Income levels played an important role during the pandemic. Frontline workers typically made less money than the general US population. On average, frontline workers made $21.95 per hour. The average American worker made $24.98 per hour.

Frontline workers in food services did not typically make much money.

Some frontline workers, such as surgeons, made much more than the national average. But most frontline workers were cashiers and food service workers. These jobs do not pay much.

Some frontline workers protested their low pay. They believed they should earn more because of the health risks of working.

In health care, frontline workers

included home health aides, nursing

assistants, cooks, and housekeepers.

The median wage for these jobs was just

$13.48 per hour. Custodians often received

less than that.

INCOME AND HOUSING

Because of these low wages, many

frontline workers didn't have the option to

stay home without working. They needed

BLACK WORKERS ON THE FRONT LINES

Black people more were likely to be hospitalized for COVID-19 than white people. This was because Black people were more likely to work on the front lines. This was especially true in certain jobs. They made up 51 percent of cashiers and 30 percent of nurses. But just 13 percent of the total US population is Black. This meant Black people were more likely than other racial groups to be exposed to COVID-19.

their paychecks to pay bills and provide for their families. If they got sick, many did not get paid sick leave. For workers in the bottom 10 percent of incomes, more than two-thirds did not have paid sick leave. Many couldn't afford to take time off, even if they weren't feeling well. Sometimes they felt they had no choice but to go to work. But going to work sick would put their coworkers at risk.

Some frontline workers lived with extended family to afford housing. Space was often tight. They could not distance from the people they lived with to keep

WORKFORCE DEMOGRAPHICS BY RACE

These pie charts compare the racial makeup of all workers to that of frontline workers based on information from 2014 through 2018. Black people made up a disproportionate percentage of frontline workers.

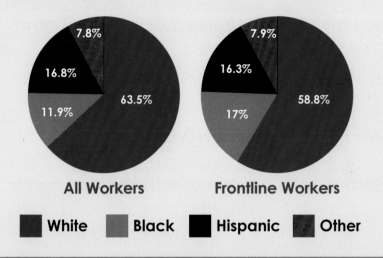

All Workers

Frontline Workers

White   Black   Hispanic   Other

Hye Jin Rho, Hayley Brown, and Shawn Fremstad, "A Basic Demographic Profile of Workers in Frontline Industries," CEPR, April 2020. www.cepr.net.

them safe. Some of those people were

at a higher risk of dying from COVID-19

because of other health issues. Sabrina

Hopps worked in housekeeping at a health

care facility. She said, "I'm petrified. . . . If I contract it, I live with my son, my daughter, and my granddaughter. My son and I have asthma. He is also a cancer survivor."[5]

IMPROVEMENTS AND DIFFICULTIES

Some frontline workers saw improvements in certain areas of their work. There was more demand for cleaning. Some custodians saw a pay raise. People realized cleaning was necessary to slow the virus.

But many people didn't see a pay raise. They felt they were risking their lives but still struggling to keep their families afloat. And more people with office jobs began working

Amazon workers saw pay raises early in the pandemic. But the higher pay was only temporary.

from home. If businesses closed offices,

they wouldn't need as many custodians.

Custodians worried they might not have

jobs anymore.

Custodians faced the pressure of being responsible for stopping the spread of the virus. Disneyland custodian Artemis Bell said, "It's scary to know, as a custodian, that if we miss the slightest little thing, someone could carry this halfway across the country."[6] Some faced this pressure along with tight time limits for cleaning. Some airlines limited cleaning crews to ten minutes. There wasn't enough time to clean all the things people touched.

Some stores raised the hourly wage for their employees. They gave bonuses to workers. But as the pandemic dragged

Many frontline workers had additional cleaning tasks during the pandemic.

on, the wages dropped again. Employees

still had to do additional tasks. They had to

sanitize counters and make sure customers

wore masks.

HAZARD PAY

Many frontline workers felt they were taking

risks far greater than their pay reflected.

They believed they should be getting

hazard pay. This is pay in addition to regular

income for work that is dangerous. Miners

and construction workers sometimes

CUSTOMERS AND MASKS

Early in the pandemic, the CDC did not recommend that the public wear masks. Scientists learned more about COVID-19. The CDC changed its recommendation. It said everyone should wear masks in public. This led some to doubt the effectiveness of masks. Frontline workers often had to enforce mask policies. A few customers became violent when reminded they needed to wear masks.

receive hazard pay. David Saucedo worked as a cook in a nursing home. He had previously been in the US Navy. He said, "When I was in the Navy, when we went to war, I was getting paid hazardous duty pay. To me, it is a hazardous job right now. We should be getting paid hazardous pay."[7]

Frontline workers often had little choice about whether they would go into work. They didn't feel safe. But they couldn't afford to stay home. They felt they were risking their lives for pay that barely supported them. They felt something needed to change.

CHAPTER FOUR

HOW DID PEOPLE HELP FRONTLINE WORKERS?

People around the country recognized the important work of frontline workers. They wanted to thank them for their hard work during the pandemic. People tried to help frontline workers do their jobs safely. They wanted to make workers' lives easier.

A message thanking frontline workers was posted in New York City.

POLITICIANS AND EMPLOYERS

Before the pandemic, the US

unemployment rate was 3.8 percent.

During the pandemic, the rate rose as high

as 14.4 percent. Some frontline workers

lost their jobs. For example, restaurant staff were at risk of losing their jobs. Many restaurants had to limit seating to keep people safe. Some had fewer customers because some people did not have the money to go out to eat as often as they once did. Others avoided restaurants for safety reasons. Restaurants did not need as many workers.

In response, the US government sent out stimulus checks in April 2020. The checks gave people money to spend at businesses. That way businesses wouldn't close. This money also helped people who

Many restaurants limited the number of customers who were allowed to dine indoors.

had lost their jobs or who were not making

much money. Individuals and families

who typically made less money received

more money from the government. The

US government also temporarily increased

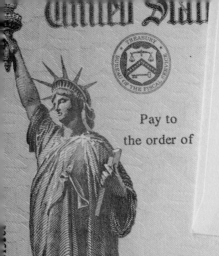

Pay to
the order of

ECONOMIC IMPACT PAYMENT
PRESIDENT DONALD J. TRUMP

The US government sent stimulus checks in April 2020 to encourage people to spend money at businesses.

the amount of money a person received on unemployment insurance. People who have lost their jobs may go on unemployment insurance. They receive payments from the government to help them while they look for new jobs.

Politicians also began working on

laws that would give hazard pay. In

May, the Democrat-controlled House of

Representatives passed an act. It included

hazard pay. The Republican-controlled

Senate rejected the bill. They said that

the $3 trillion act was too expensive. The

House passed a new $2.2 trillion act in

October. The Senate again rejected it.

Senate Republicans instead introduced

their own $1 trillion bill. This bill included

stimulus money. But it did not have hazard

pay. Democrats did not support the bill.

Republicans and Democrats continued

On Election Day in 2020, people in Florida voted to increase minimum wage to fifteen dollars an hour.

negotiating a second stimulus bill that would work for both parties.

Some city governments increased pay for frontline employees. Atlanta, Georgia, raised its frontline workers' salaries by $500 per month. In July, the state of Louisiana opened applications for a one-time payment of $250 for frontline workers. Nurses, cops, and store clerks were among those who could apply. Some employers also raised frontline workers' pay. Target, Amazon, Kroger, and other companies raised hourly pay by two dollars an hour. However, that still did not give some people enough to meet their basic needs. Lisa Harris worked at Kroger in Virginia. She said of the pay increase, "I don't think that is enough, especially for those who started off at minimum wage. And it is only temporary during this crisis. . . . We are heroes every day, and we deserve to be paid as such. We haven't gone from unskilled labor to essential personnel. We always were essential personnel."[8]

HEROES HEALTH APP

The University of North Carolina released the Heroes Health app in July 2020. The app aimed to help health care workers with their mental wellness. Every week the app would help users assess any mental health symptoms. It asked about sleeping patterns, stress levels, and whether they were experiencing depression. The app provided users with resources they could use to help their mental health.

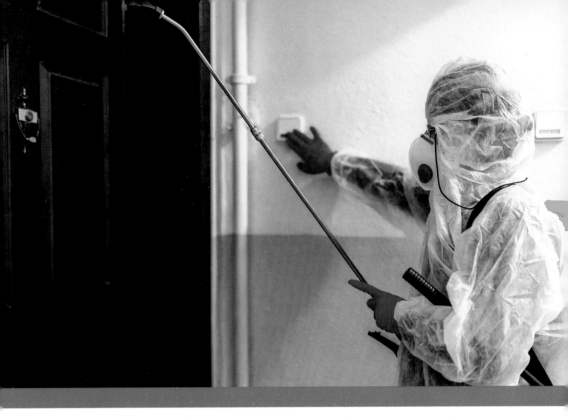

Some custodians were given special equipment to make cleaning faster.

HELPFUL TOOLS

Employers made other changes to

help frontline workers. In many places,

custodians had to clean more frequently.

This took more time. Employers purchased

tools to help custodians work faster.

Some purchased disinfectant sprayers.

In the past, if there was a flu outbreak,

custodians would have to clean entire

classrooms by hand. With the sprayer, they

could disinfect a whole room in minutes.

Researchers looked for other ways

to help frontline workers. They began

training dogs to detect people infected

with COVID-19. Dogs cannot smell the

virus itself. But the body makes a unique

combination of odors when it is infected.

Researchers taught dogs to detect this

unique scent. Dogs could even smell the

disease before people showed symptoms.

A specially trained dog in the Helsinki Airport was able to identify visitors who had COVID-19.

The Helsinki Airport in Finland began

offering voluntary COVID-19 tests in

September 2020. These tests were done

by dogs. People entering the country were

encouraged to get tested. They would use a

cloth to wipe some of their sweat. A trained

CARE COVE

Steven Tropello is a doctor in Baltimore,
Maryland. In March 2020, he used a garbage
bag to protect himself. There were not enough
gowns. He began designing the Care Cove.
It was a clear material that could be wrapped
around patients, forming a bubble. It had
sleeves that health care workers could use.
They could reach in to care for the patient. This
kept the virus from spreading from the patient.

dog would smell it. If the dog signaled that the person was infected, the person could go to the hospital to confirm. Airport staff were alerted if they may have been exposed to the virus. The staff could get tested too. Fewer people were exposed when the virus was found early.

HELP FROM THE PUBLIC

The public also helped frontline workers. People who were doing well financially gave large tips to restaurant workers. Some people used their stimulus checks to give tips too.

Some people had N95 masks at the beginning of the pandemic. They donated the masks to hospitals. They wanted doctors and nurses to stay protected. Other people sewed cloth masks to donate to hospitals. These masks were given to health care workers who did not have direct contact with COVID-19 patients. The N95 masks could be saved for people who were directly exposed to COVID-19. Cloth masks could also be worn over N95 masks. This helped keep the N95 masks clean for extended use. Volunteer Sabrina Roffman said, "We want people in the

Some people made homemade masks to donate to frontline workers.

hospital . . . to know that they're not in this

by themselves."[9]

Some people volunteered to

provide childcare for frontline workers.

Many schools and day cares were closed.

Grocery deliveries were helpful for frontline workers who did not have time to shop for themselves.

Some frontline workers had no one to

care for their children while they worked.

Organizations such as MN COVIDsitters

in Minnesota paired students with frontline

workers. Workers wouldn't have to worry

about childcare. People also volunteered to shop for health care workers. Workers exposed to COVID-19 did not want to go to stores. They could expose others. Sometimes they worked extra hours. Time for grocery shopping was hard to fit in. Volunteers shopped for them.

Frontline workers faced many challenges during the pandemic. But there were people who tried to help make their jobs a little easier. Together they faced the challenges of the pandemic and worked for a better future.

GLOSSARY

contagious
able to spread by direct or indirect contact

custodians
people who clean and take care of buildings

exposed
put at risk of a harmful condition or action

federal
having to do with a country's government at the national level

mandates
orders or commands

pandemic
an outbreak of disease that occurs over a wide area

stockpile
a supply of an item held for future use

symptoms
the effects that a person feels from a disease

unemployment
the state of being without a job

SOURCE NOTES

INTRODUCTION: WHO ARE FRONTLINE WORKERS?

1. Quoted in Eric Boodman, "In the COVID-19 Death of a Hospital Food Worker, A Microcosm of the Pandemic," *Stat*, June 30, 2020. www.statnews.com.

CHAPTER ONE: HOW WERE FRONTLINE WORKERS AT HIGH RISK?

2. Quoted in Brad Streicher, "Austin ISD Custodians Say Moving Campuses Is Causing COVID-19 to Spread," *KVUE*, July 1, 2020. www.kvue.com.

CHAPTER TWO: HOW DO FRONTLINE WORKERS PROTECT THEMSELVES?

3. Quoted in Molly Kinder, "Meet the COVID-19 Frontline Heroes," *Brookings*, May 2020. www.brookings.edu.

4. Quoted in Emma Grey Ellis, "How Health Care Workers Avoid Bringing Covid-19 Home," *Wired*, April 14, 2020. www.wired.com.

CHAPTER THREE: HOW DID INCOME LEVEL AFFECT WORKERS?

5. Quoted in Molly Kinder, "COVID-19's Essential Workers Deserve Hazard Pay," *Brookings*, April 10, 2020. www.brookings.edu.

6. Quoted in Jodi Kantor, "No Bleach and Dirty Rags," *New York Times*, July 20, 2020. www.nytimes.com.

7. Quoted in Molly Kinder, "Essential but Undervalued," *Brookings*, May 28, 2020. www.brookings.edu.

CHAPTER FOUR: HOW DID PEOPLE HELP FRONTLINE WORKERS?

8. Quoted in Kinder, "COVID-19's Essential Workers Deserve Hazard Pay."

9. Quoted in Maxine Lipner, "Volunteers Work with Hospitals to Make Emergency Face Masks for Workers," *Today*, March 31, 2020. www.today.com.

FOR FURTHER RESEARCH

BOOKS

Heather DiLorenzo Williams, *Essential Workers, Essential Heroes*. Minneapolis, MN: Lerner, 2021.

Martha London, *Flattening the Curve*. Minneapolis, MN: Abdo, 2021.

Walt K. Moon, *The COVID-19 Virus*. San Diego, CA: BrightPoint, 2021.

INTERNET SOURCES

"Looking After Our Mental Health," *World Health Organization*, n.d. www.who.int.

"What Is Coronavirus?" *Johns Hopkins Medicine*, November 5, 2020. www.hopkinsmedicine.org.

"Work That Is Vital, Workers Who Are Essential," *Harvard Gazette*, November 2, 2020. https://news.harvard.edu.

WEBSITES

Brookings Institution: COVID-19 Frontline Heroes
www.brookings.edu/interactives/meet-the-covid-19-frontline
-heroes

The Brookings Institution is a nonprofit public policy organization that researches issues society faces at the local, national, and global levels.

Mayo Clinic
www.mayoclinic.org

Mayo Clinic is a nonprofit health organization that provides medical care and resources to people across the United States.

National Institute of Mental Health
www.nimh.nih.gov

The National Institute of Mental Health (NIMH) is a government agency that conducts research into mental health and public health issues, including how COVID-19 has impacted Americans' mental health.

INDEX

IMAGE CREDITS

ABOUT THE AUTHOR

Kerry Dinmont is a children's book author who enjoys art and nature. She lives in Montana with her two Norwegian elkhounds.